# ADAM and FAMILY

Written by Russell Grigg

Illustrated by Caleb Salisbury

ISBN: 9781921643460
First printing 2011

Published and distributed by

CREATION
BOOK PUBLISHERS

www.creationbookpublishers.com

# Hey Kids!

Did you know that you are related to every other person in the world, regardless of where they live, what colour their skin is, or what language they speak! This is because we all have the very same great, great, great ... great, great, great ... grandparents, who were called Adam and Eve.

You may have heard that people evolved from apes. Well, that is not true. Adam and Eve didn't evolve from apes. God created them both, Adam first and then Eve. They formed the very first family in the world, and everybody who has ever lived has been descended from them.

Have you ever wondered why there is so much pain and suffering in the world? And even why we have to die? This book tells what Adam and Eve did that caused these things to happen. It also tells how God can help you live in a right relationship with Him. He loves you, and He wants you to love him too.

Happy reading!

For some activities related to these pages see creationforkids.com/activity

# ADAM'S FIRST TASK:
# NAMING
## THE ANIMALS

**A**FTER God created Adam on Day 6 of Creation Week, He had a very special task for Adam to do. It was to name the birds and some of the land animals that God had created before He made Adam.

Adam lived in a wonderful parkland called the Garden of Eden. Eden means "a beautiful place". Nowadays we don't know where this was, because it was later destroyed by Noah's Flood. There were all kinds of fruit trees and plants there, which provided delicious food for Adam and the animals.

Adam lived in a very different world from what we see today. All the birds, which God had created on Day 5, and all the animals, which God had created on Day 6, were harmless. This included the dinosaurs. The animals ate fruit and vegetation and did not fight or kill each other.

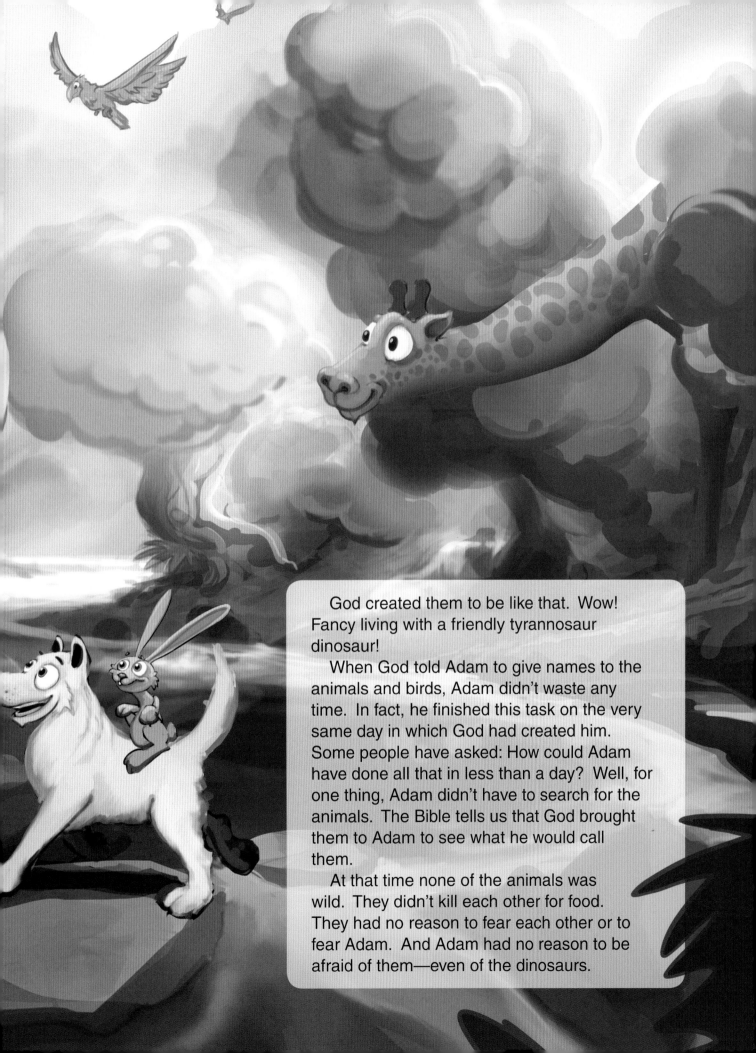

God created them to be like that. Wow! Fancy living with a friendly tyrannosaur dinosaur!

When God told Adam to give names to the animals and birds, Adam didn't waste any time. In fact, he finished this task on the very same day in which God had created him. Some people have asked: How could Adam have done all that in less than a day? Well, for one thing, Adam didn't have to search for the animals. The Bible tells us that God brought them to Adam to see what he would call them.

At that time none of the animals was wild. They didn't kill each other for food. They had no reason to fear each other or to fear Adam. And Adam had no reason to be afraid of them—even of the dinosaurs.

# 'Kinds' of animals

The Bible uses the word 'kinds', rather than 'species', to describe the different birds and animals. Today there are several species of dog (wolf, jackal, coyote, dingo and the domestic breeds) within the dog kind, and several species of bear (black, grizzly, polar, and brown) within the bear kind, and so on. So Adam did not have to name millions of animals. Naming each kind was enough. Adam had to name only:

## 1. The livestock,

like sheep, cattle, pigs, rabbits, horses and camels. Probably less than a dozen kinds.

## 2. The birds.

There are about 2,400 species of birds, which scientists group into 165 'families'. (A bird 'family' is probably the same as a Genesis 'kind'.) This includes all those living today and those known from fossils to be extinct. One of these 'kinds', the parrot family, today is made up of over 300 species. So if Adam named each group with its general name, such as 'ducks', 'gulls' and 'owls', there would have been fewer than 200 kinds of birds for him to name.

# 3. The beasts of the field.

These probably lived in open country. Adam wasn't told to name all 'the beasts of the earth' mentioned in Genesis 1:24, but just 'the beasts of the field' (Genesis 2:19). He did not have to name any creepy crawlies, or any fish. Did you know that only 2% of all creatures are animals with backbones? (And most of these are fish.) They are called 'vertebrates'.

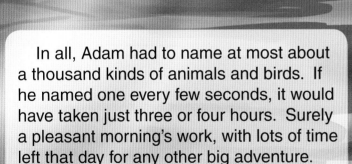

In all, Adam had to name at most about a thousand kinds of animals and birds. If he named one every few seconds, it would have taken just three or four hours. Surely a pleasant morning's work, with lots of time left that day for any other big adventure.

### Was Adam equal to the task?

Adam was not a stooped, dim-witted, grunting ape-man that God zapped to make into the first human being. How do we know? The Bible does not say that man evolved from apes or any other animal, but God took some dust and made the first man.

Also, it says that among all the animals there was not one that was a suitable helper, or mate, for Adam. Not one was like him, because God had made him in God's own image, not in the image of an ape. This means that Adam was a person. He had a spiritual nature—he was able to talk to God, and understand God when God talked to him.

At the naming parade, Adam used the language God had programmed him to speak. With his high intelligence, he could have said one or two words to describe each animal, without confusion or repetition, and without forgetting what names he had already used.

You too have a spiritual nature. This means that you can talk to God in prayer. God wants you to do this. He has things He wants to say to you, too. Every day you can read what God says to you in the Bible. Why not read it today?

# She's Beautiful!

**A**DAM WAS THE only human in existence. In the beautiful parkland called the Garden of Eden where he lived, he had all the animals he wanted for pets. But they all had mates, and he did not—he was all alone. God had given Adam the task of naming the animals. Adam finished the task very quickly. But then he realized even more how different he was from every one of them, including the apes. None of them could talk to him. None of them could share the times when he talked with God. None of them was a suitable mate for Adam.

## A wife for Adam

God knew that Adam was alone and needed a mate. So God did something very, very special. He put Adam into a deep, deep sleep. Then God took one of Adam's ribs and used it to make the first woman.

When Adam woke up, not only was his side all closed up and healed, but there beside him was another person. And she was beautiful!

The Bible tells us that Adam later named her Eve, which means 'life', because she would become the mother of all people on Earth (Genesis 3:20).

Because of Eve you are related to every person who is living today or who has ever lived. You and they all have the same great, great, great … great, great, great … grandmother—Eve. And we all have the same great, great, great … great, great, great … grandfather—Adam. This is one huge reason why no-one should ever look down on any other person who may have different-coloured skin, or is different in any other way. We are all related!

Adam and Eve were the very first husband and wife. Marriage of one man to one woman for life is something that God invented. He didn't create Adam and Steve, because He didn't want men to marry men. He didn't create Tammie and Eve, because He didn't want women to marry women. And God didn't want a man or a woman to have several partners, because He created only one man and one woman at the beginning. God's way for us to live is always best.

# No Ape-Men ever!

Some people have said that, before Adam lived, there were 'ape-men'. But this is not true. There never have been any half-ape, half-humans, because evolution is not true. God did not make Adam from an ape. The Bible tells us that God made the first humans in His own image and likeness, not in the image and likeness of an ape.

Over the years, people have looked for 'missing links' and come up with all sorts of funny ideas. Like Piltdown Man. Someone found a piece of a human skull and the lower jaw of an orangutan at a place called Piltdown, in England,

in 1912. For 40 years, evolutionists declared that these bones were a 'missing link' between men and apes. Then, in 1953, it was all shown to be a hoax!

In 1922, someone in Nebraska, USA, found a tooth. A scientist gave it a scientific name, an artist in England drew a picture of an ape-like man and his wife, and Nebraska Man was created. A few years later, it was found out that the tooth was from an animal like a pig!

In 1974, part of a skeleton, about one metre (3 ft) tall, was found in Ethiopia. The bones were called 'Lucy' because, at

the time they were found, the loudspeaker at the camp was playing the Beatles' song, 'Lucy in the Sky with Diamonds'. 'Lucy' has been shown in museums looking like an ape-woman, with ape-like face and head, and human-like hands and feet. However, the bones found did not include the upper jaw and most of the skull, or the hand and foot bones. They are just the bones of a kind of ape.

There are varieties of apes and of humans. There are no half-way forms. All the 'missing links' are still missing— because they never existed!

# Choices, Choices

DO YOU have rules in your home, like keeping your room tidy or being on time for meals? Do you think rules are a good idea?

God had just one rule for Adam in the beautiful garden He had given him to be his home. He told Adam that he could eat the fruit from any of the trees in the Garden of Eden, except one, which God called the Tree of the Knowledge of Good and Evil. He also warned Adam that if he did eat from that tree he would die (Genesis 2:8–9; 15–17).

Why did God give Adam a rule like that? If you have a computer, you could program it to display the words "I love you" on the screen. Or if you are playing with a puppet, you can make the puppet say, "I love you". But would that mean that the computer or the puppet loved you? No, of course not. Why not? Because neither the computer nor the puppet has a choice. They can do only what they are programmed to do or made to say.

God wanted Adam, and Eve too, to *choose* to love and obey Him. But for this to happen, they also had to be free to disobey Him, if they wanted to. Otherwise they wouldn't have had a choice! God didn't want them to be like a computer, or like puppets, when it came to loving Him.

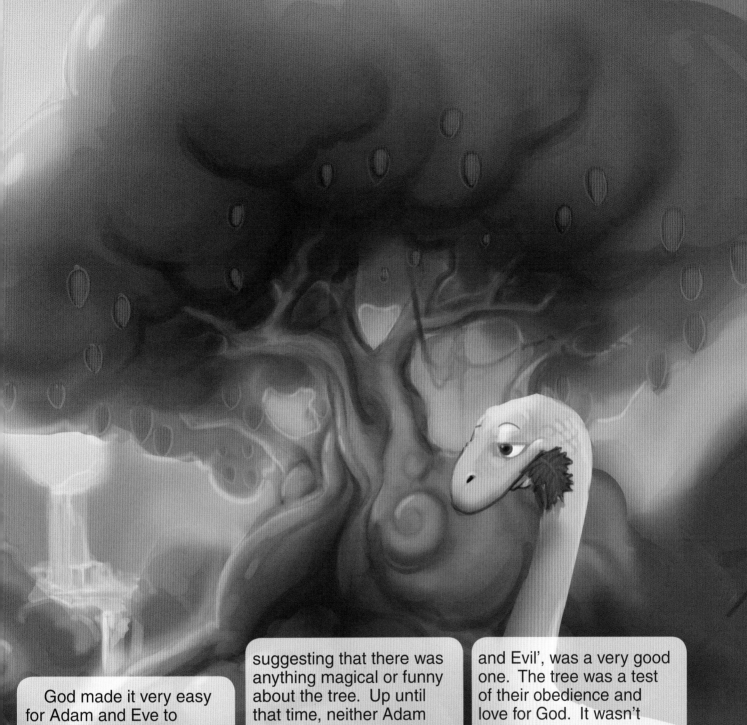

God made it very easy for Adam and Eve to choose to obey Him by giving them lots and lots of lovely trees to eat the fruit from. He made it quite hard for them to choose to disobey Him, because there was only one tree in the whole garden that God had said they couldn't eat from.

You might wonder why the tree had such a weird name. Well, we are not suggesting that there was anything magical or funny about the tree. Up until that time, neither Adam nor Eve had done anything wrong. So there was no sin in the world. Adam and Eve knew only about things that were good. Now, God was letting them know that, if they ate the fruit from that tree, they would be disobeying Him, and so they would find out what 'evil' was.

So the name, 'the Tree of the Knowledge of Good and Evil', was a very good one. The tree was a test of their obedience and love for God. It wasn't poisonous. It was 'very good', like everything else that God had made. Death was the penalty Adam and Eve would pay if they disobeyed God and did what He had told them not to do.

Did God have the right to give them this rule, and set such a huge penalty if they disobeyed Him? Yes. Do you like to play the game called Monopoly? Well, the creator of the game of Monopoly had the right to decide the rules and penalties of the game he created. As Adam and Eve's Creator, God had the right to set any rules He chose for them to obey. In the same way, God has the right to set the rules of life for us to obey, too.

Nowadays you may hear some people say, "There is no difference between right and wrong," or "Whatever you want to do, if it feels good, do it." God says that there *is* a difference between right and wrong, and He is the One who decides what that difference is. When we do wrong things it is called 'sin'. So sin is anything we think, or say, or do, in disobedience to God.

God didn't make up His rules to keep us from enjoying ourselves. God loves you, and He wants you to love Him, and to obey Him, and to trust Him. So His rules are for our protection, like "Don't murder", "Don't steal", "Don't lie", and so on.

God does not want us to find out what evil is like by experimenting with it. If we do, we may soon find out that we can't stop thinking, or saying, or doing that thing. Do you know of someone who decided to experiment with cigarettes, and now can't stop smoking? They have become a slave to their habit. It's like that with sin generally.

When you are tempted to do something you know is wrong, God is giving you the opportunity to choose either to obey Him or to disobey Him. However, you can't easily do this by yourself; you need God's help. When you receive Jesus as your Saviour and Lord, God gives you the Holy Spirit to live in you and to help you choose to obey God and not to sin.

RIGHT STREET

# Temptation

ADAM AND EVE greatly enjoyed living in the beautiful place, called the Garden of Eden, which God had given them to be their home. They liked eating the delicious fruit, looking after things, and playing with the animals. God had said that they could eat the fruit from any tree in the garden, except from the Tree of the Knowledge of Good and Evil. He had warned them that, if they ate from that one, they would die.

One day, Eve heard someone speaking to her. The voice was coming from the direction of a snake. Who could it be? It was Satan, the devil. Satan was using the snake to speak to Eve.

"Did God *really* say you must not eat any of the fruit from these lovely trees?" he asked.

"Of course not," Eve replied. "We can eat all the fruit we want—except for just that one tree over there." Eve then told Satan that God had said they must not eat or touch the fruit, otherwise they would die. (Actually, God had only said not to *eat* the fruit.)

"That's not true," said Satan. "God knows that if you eat that fruit you will be like God, knowing good and evil." But Satan was lying.

Eve looked at the fruit. How beautiful it was! She thought how nice it would taste, and how good it would be to be wise. She grabbed some, took a big juicy bite, and gave some to Adam, who ate some too.

Immediately Adam and Eve knew that they had done something wrong. Now they knew what evil was! Evil, they realized, was disobeying God. They felt guilty and ashamed. It dawned on them that it was not God who had lied to them, but Satan. They didn't feel the marvellous result that Satan had promised. Sin is always like this. We think we will enjoy doing something we know

is wrong, but then we find that it causes us shame and regret. Suddenly they were very afraid to meet God.

Later that day, when God came to the garden, they hid from Him among the trees. This didn't do any good, because no-one can hide from God. God called out, "Where are you, Adam?" With heads bent they crept out into the open and stood before God.

God asked them if they had eaten the fruit from the Tree of the Knowledge of Good and Evil. God knew they had, but did Adam own up? No! Instead, he made an excuse and tried to blame someone else.

"It was not *my* fault," Adam said. "Eve persuaded me."

"It was not *my* fault," Eve said. "The snake tricked me into eating it."

God then told the snake that it was cursed and that it and the woman's descendants would be enemies. One of her descendants would bruise its head, and it would bruise his heel. This was a prophecy. It referred to the fact that God's Son, the Lord Jesus Christ, would come to Earth. He would defeat the work of Satan through His death on the Cross and Resurrection.

God still loved Adam and Eve. However, He told Eve that, because of what she had done, she would have great pain in child-bearing. Yet, her daughters (and their daughters) would still want to have husbands. God told Adam that, because of what he had done, the ground was now under a curse. It would produce weeds and thorns. Adam would have to dig the ground and work hard to make it produce food all his lifetime. Then he would die, and his body would return to dust.

The Bible tells us that God made clothes out of animal skins for Adam and Eve, to replace the fig-leaves they had put on when they tried to hide from God. This means that at least one animal must have died—all because of what Adam did.

Then God expelled Adam and Eve from the garden, so they would not eat from

another tree there called the Tree of Life, and live for ever. He put an angel on guard to stop them from ever returning. Adam and Eve were cut off from the close contact they had enjoyed with God in the garden.

From that time on, they began to die, even though they would live on for many more years. This was what God had said would happen, when He warned them not to eat from that tree.

When Jesus was on Earth, Satan tried to tempt Him to do wrong things (Matthew 4:1–11). Jesus resisted Satan's temptations by quoting verses from the Bible. When we are tempted, the Bible promises that God will give us a way of escape (1 Corinthians 10:13). It also tells us to submit to God, and that, if we resist the devil, he will flee from us (James 4:7). How many verses from the Bible do you know?

The **FALL**

A LESSON NEVER TO FORGET!

HAVE YOU EVER wondered why there is so much suffering in the world, so much sickness, so much killing, so many wars? The Bible gives us the answer. It tells us that when God made Adam and Eve, they lived in a world where there was no suffering, no sickness and no death. Even the animals all ate plants and not each other. This included the dinosaurs. Then, as a test of Adam and Eve's loyalty and love for Him, God allowed them to be tempted by Satan.

In the Garden of Eden, Satan wanted to get Eve to disobey God. Somehow he had to get her to eat some fruit from the Tree of the Knowledge of Good and Evil. Why? Because that was the one thing that God had told Adam not to do, on penalty of death. Satan had a very cunning plan to drag her down.

The Bible tells us that there is a supremely evil being in the universe, whose name is Satan. He is also called the tempter, the accuser, the deceiver of the whole world, the father of lies, and that old serpent the devil (Revelation 12:9; 20:2).

He was created a very special angel, who was very beautiful, very powerful and very intelligent. Then he became proud and rebelled against God. Because of this, he was cast out of Heaven. He is now called Satan, meaning 'adversary', or the devil. Many other angels followed him (Matthew 25:41).

What does Satan look like? We can't be sure. The Bible tells us he can disguise himself as an angel of light (2 Corinthians 11:14). However, he is an evil angel, who is now the enemy of God. He tries to tempt people to rebel against God just as he did, to sin, and do all kinds of wrong things—just like we see going on in the world today.

# Who is Satan?

First of all, he cast doubt on what God had said about not eating the fruit. Then he denied that Eve would die if she did eat it. Then he told Eve that the fruit was something really nice and that God was unfair in keeping her from enjoying it. In fact, he told her that God was being selfish—He didn't want her to eat the fruit because then she would be like Him.

To experience this, Eve would have to ignore the penalty that God had warned them of, but Satan didn't let her think about that. How tricky! And it worked. Eve believed what Satan had said, instead of what God had said. She and Adam both ate the fruit that God had told them not to.

Now you might think it was a very small thing just to eat a piece of fruit like that. Why should it involve such a huge penalty? No less than death! Well, what Adam and Eve did was rebellion against God. They wanted to decide what was good and what was evil for themselves. They wanted life without

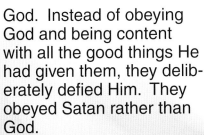

God. Instead of obeying God and being content with all the good things He had given them, they deliberately defied Him. They obeyed Satan rather than God.

Because God is perfectly holy and just, there had to be a penalty for rebellion, or sin, against Him. The penalty ('Curse') involved death, because that was what God had warned them would happen if they disobeyed Him. When God judged sin, He also withdrew some of His sustaining power in the world. This first sin, with its penalty, is called 'the Fall'. Because of sin, we now have a 'fallen' world with suffering, sickness, calamities and death. People are violent because that's what they choose to be.

God often deals with sin by allowing people to have what they want, but there are always consequences. Adam and Eve ate the fruit, and from then on they were cut off from God, the source of all goodness and light, and of life itself.

## What the Fall means for us today

All of us are descended from Adam, who was the head of the human race. We have all been born with an anti-God nature from Adam. And Satan's strategy today is still the same as it was in the Garden of Eden—he casts doubt on the Word of God, and denies its truth. Satan tempts us to disregard what it says, and wants us to think that there is no penalty for sin.

However, God has not forsaken us. Because He loves us, God sent His Son, the Lord Jesus Christ, to pay the penalty for our sins by His death on the Cross. Because the penalty has been paid, God can now forgive us for our sin (1 John 1:9), free us from guilt, and restore us to a right relationship with Himself. When Jesus rose from the dead, He showed that death had been conquered (1 Corinthians 15:20–26). All we have to 'do' is turn to God and ask Him to forgive our sin and to be our Saviour and our Lord.

The message of the Bible is that, although we are in a war with Satan, in Christ our victory has already been won! We have a choice: to sin and obey Satan, or to accept Jesus Christ as our Saviour and obey Him.

# Cain and the First Murder

AFTER ADAM AND EVE were expelled from the Garden of Eden for their rebellion against God, they began having a family. Their first child was a boy, whom they named Cain. Then they had another boy, whom they named Abel. When the boys grew up, Cain became a farmer and grew crops, and Abel became a shepherd.

### Making an offering to God

One day each of them brought an offering to God. Cain brought some of the fruit he Had grown, but Abel offered the very best lamb in his flock. We can imagine that they each made an altar out of stones, put some wood on it, set fire to the wood, and placed their offerings on top of the fire. God was pleased with Abel and with his offering, which cost the life of the lamb he offered. However, God was not pleased with Cain or of the offering of fruit that Cain had made.

Why the difference? Jesus called Abel a righteous man (Matthew 23:35). The Bible says that Abel made his offering by faith (Hebrews 11:4), and it says that faith comes from hearing God's word (Romans 10:17). So perhaps God had told the family what He wanted them to do, and the sort of offering He wanted

them to make when they came to Him. Perhaps too their father, Adam, had told them about the time when he and Eve had disobeyed God, and how God had made clothes of animal skin to replace the fig leaves they were wearing. This means that at least one animal had died because of Adam and Eve's sin.

Cain disregarded all this. He could have traded some of his fruit for one

of Abel's lambs, but it seems he didn't want to do things God's way. Instead, he wanted to decide for himself how he would behave, and what was right and what was wrong as far as he was concerned. His heart was not right towards God.

When God rejected Cain's offering, Cain was very angry. God said to him, "Why are you angry and downcast, Cain? If you do what's right will you not be accepted? But if you don't do what's right, sin is like a wild animal crouching at your door. It wants to have you, but you must overcome it."

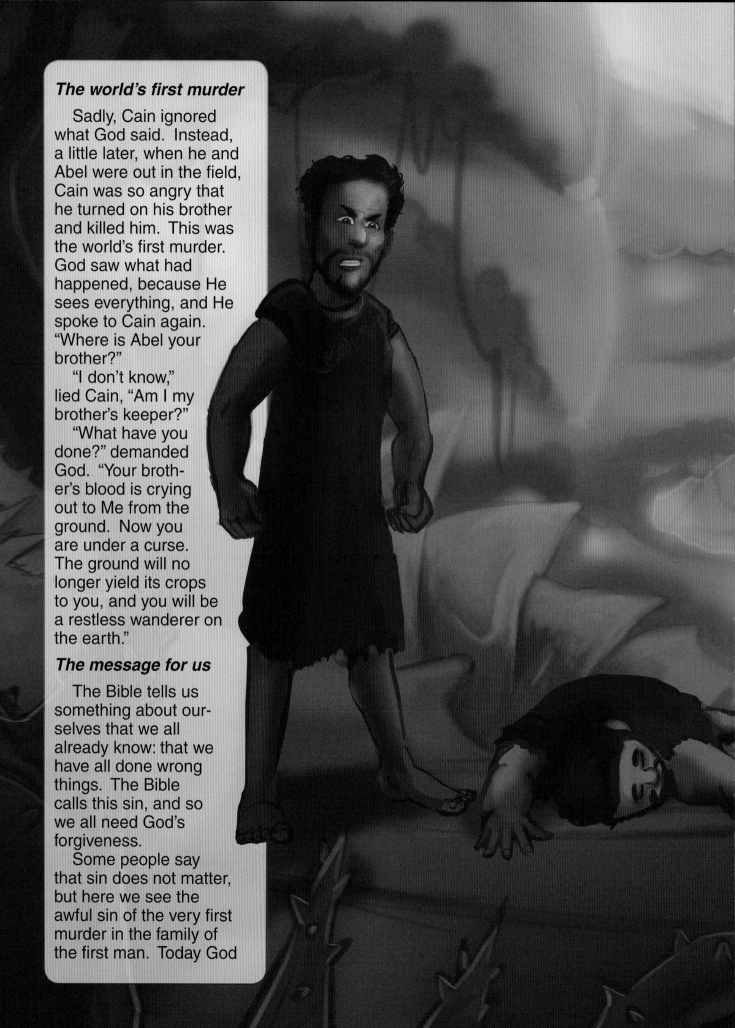

### The world's first murder

Sadly, Cain ignored what God said. Instead, a little later, when he and Abel were out in the field, Cain was so angry that he turned on his brother and killed him. This was the world's first murder. God saw what had happened, because He sees everything, and He spoke to Cain again. "Where is Abel your brother?"

"I don't know," lied Cain, "Am I my brother's keeper?"

"What have you done?" demanded God. "Your brother's blood is crying out to Me from the ground. Now you are under a curse. The ground will no longer yield its crops to you, and you will be a restless wanderer on the earth."

### The message for us

The Bible tells us something about ourselves that we all already know: that we have all done wrong things. The Bible calls this sin, and so we all need God's forgiveness.

Some people say that sin does not matter, but here we see the awful sin of the very first murder in the family of the first man. Today God doesn't want people to make blood sacrifices like the lamb Abel offered. God has already done this for us through the death of His Son, the Lord Jesus Christ, on the Cross. Jesus is called 'the lamb of God'. This is because when Jesus died, He shed His blood for us, as 'a once for all' sacrifice. This paid the penalty for everyone's sins (Hebrews 10:10; 1 Peter 1:18–19). Because of this, God can now justly forgive all those who are willing to receive His forgiveness, His gift of salvation.

*'For God so loved the world, that he gave His only Son, that whoever believes in Him should not perish, but have eternal life'* (John 3:16).

However, Jesus didn't stay dead. He came back to life and now sits at the right hand of God the Father, in Heaven. He came to Earth for our sake, and He is the only One who has ever resisted Satan's temptations without ever sinning. When we are tempted to do things we know are wrong, we can ask Jesus to help us overcome the temptation, because He can give us the power to do so and live lives that are pleasing to God. The Bible says,

*'God is faithful, and He will not let you be tempted beyond your ability, but with the temptation He will also provide the way of escape, that you may be able to endure it.'* (1 Corinthians 10:13).

When Jesus was tempted He resisted Satan by remembering verses from the Bible. How many Bible verses do you know? See if you can memorize the two verses given above.

# CAIN'S WIFE WHO WAS SHE?

AFTER CAIN killed his brother Abel, he moved to a place called Nod. Here he and his wife had a son whom they named Enoch. In time, there were enough people there to build a 'city' (Genesis 4:17), which Cain also called Enoch after his first son.

So who was Mrs Cain? And who were all those other people?

Reading the Bible gives us the answer. Adam and Eve were the very first two people. They had "other sons and daughters" besides Cain and Abel (Genesis 5:3–5), and one of these they named Seth. We are not told the names of the others, but as Adam lived for 930 years, there were lots and lots of them. Remember, God had commanded Adam and Eve "to be fruitful and multiply and fill the earth" (Genesis 1:28).

At the beginning of human history, Adam's sons—Cain, Seth and their brothers—must have married their own sisters. This is because Adam and Eve were the parents of everyone. After that, their children's sons could have married their sisters or their girl cousins, and had children of their own. Very soon, there would have been hundreds of people living on the earth. And then thousands. And soon hundreds of thousands.

Evolutionists say that

# They were clever!

once upon a time there were ape-men, and then the first humans were dumb cavemen. This is not true. There never were any ape-men. And the first people weren't dumb either. They were very clever.

The Bible says a man named Jabal was the first of those who live in tents and look after livestock—animals such as cattle, horses and camels, as well as Abel's sheep. His brother, Jubal, was very smart; he invented the harp and the flute. It takes a lot of know-how to make a harp, and a flute too, as well as to play them.

Another man, named Tubal-cain, was also an inventor—he was famous for making all kinds of tools out of bronze and iron (Genesis 4:20–22). This meant he knew how to extract copper, tin and iron from their ores.

All of this culture, such as farming, making music, and using tools, is proof that the very first people on Earth were not ape-men, and not dumb 'cavemen' either. Civilization existed from the very first—not millions or billions of years after God created the earth.

# Can brothers marry their sisters today?

But isn't it against the law now for brothers to marry their sisters? Why would it have been all right back then?

To answer, let's first consider the world today. If brothers marry their sisters, then their children may be deformed or sick or handicapped in some way. This is because in our genes, we all have some 'copying mistakes' that have built up in our family over many generations.

Different families have different copying mistakes. When people with *different* gene mistakes marry, the good genes from each partner tend to override the other partner's bad genes, so that deformities do not appear in their children. But if people with the *same* gene mistakes marry, then their children are liable to inherit two sets of bad genes, and so they can be handicapped in some way.

This was not a problem for Adam and Eve's children, because God created Adam and Eve perfect, with no genetic mistakes! So there was no problem with brothers marrying sisters.

But then, when sin entered the world, God withdrew some of His power that stopped things from falling apart. His perfect creation began to degenerate. There was death and decay, and all sorts of genetic mistakes began to develop in living things. This was minimal at the time of Cain, so intermarriage was okay, but by the time of Moses, 2,500 years later, genetic mistakes had built up to the point where it became necessary for God to forbid brothers from marrying their own sisters (Leviticus 18:1–18). That's why it was okay at the beginning, but is not okay today to marry your close relative.

## Activity
See how far back you can trace your own family tree. Ask your parents and grandparents for names and dates, and for photos that you can paste in an exercise book showing your own ancestors.

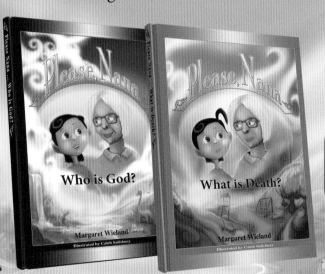